FERAL

Kate Potts is a London-based poet, academic and editor. She teaches poetry and creative writing for the University of Oxford, Middlesex University and The Poetry School, freelances as a mentor and editor, and works for an independent publisher. She completed a practice-based PhD on the poetic radio play in 2017.

Her pamphlet *Whichever Music* (tall-lighthouse) was a Poetry Book Society Pamphlet Choice in 2008 and was shortlisted for a Michael Marks Award. Her first full-length collection, *Pure Hustle*, was published by Bloodaxe in 2011. Her second collection, *Feral* (Bloodaxe Books, 2018), is a Poetry Book Society Recommendation.

Kate is co-director of Somewhere in Particular, a site-specific poetry organisation which aims to connect poetry performance to specific places and communities and to reach beyond conventional audiences.

KATE POTTS

FERAL

BLOODAXE BOOKS

ISBN: 978 1 78037 416 1

First published 2018 by
Bloodaxe Books Ltd,
Eastburn,
South Park,
Hexham,
Northumberland NE46 1BS.

www.bloodaxebooks.com
For further information about Bloodaxe titles
please visit our website or write to
the above address for a catalogue.

Supported using public funding by
ARTS COUNCIL
ENGLAND

Printed in Great Britain by Bell & Bain Limited, Glasgow, Scotland, on
acid-free paper sourced from mills with FSC chain of custody certification.

For my sisters

ACKNOWLEDGEMENTS

I'm grateful to the editors of the following publications, in which some of these poems previously appeared: *Coin Opera 2: Fulminare's Revenge* (Sidekick Books, 2013), *Cycle Lifestyle, Disclosure Magazine, The Emma Press Anthology of Love* (The Emma Press, 2018), *The Harlequin, MAP: Poems After William Smith's Geological Map of 1815 (Worple Press, 2015), Magma Poetry, Poems in Which, Poetry, The Poetry Review, Poetry Wales, Ploughshares, Prac Crit, The Tree Line: Poems for Trees, Woods & People* (Worple Press, 2017), *Under the Radar, Visual Verse* and *The White Review*.

For invaluable support, advice, solidarity and occasional epic karaoke sessions I'm deeply grateful to Alison Winch, Dai George, Kayo Chingonyi, Holly Hopkins, Sarah Howe, Jon Stone, Abigail Parry, Nia Davies, Rowena Knight, John McCullough, Amy Evans and John Canfield. Thanks also to Generative Constraints Committee, to Cath Drake, Peter Daniels and all at Poetry Booth, and to James Goodman, Nicola Collett, Kristin Linklater, Neil Astley, Roddy Lumsden, Robert Hampson, and Jo Shapcott. I am grateful to the Hawthornden Foundation for a writing fellowship, and to Arts Council England for an award towards the writing of this book.

CONTENTS

Animal Song

from **The Blown Definitions**

Postscript

ANIMAL SONG

The cultural marginalisation of animals is, of course, a more
complex process than their physical marginalisation. The animals
of the mind cannot be so easily dispersed.

JOHN BERGER

Thirty-three

Now all the boys I've loved are married off, ensconced.
They bide in milky, clean-hewn terraces, in replicated seaside towns.

They wear matched socks. They wash. They see their own fathers' chins
and petulance – the kindnesses and tics – grow strong

and coarse in them, and this is comfort. They lullaby
their round-faced wives in lusty, baritone, newsreader voices.

Pour me a slug of this late August clarity of light: the contrast turned up high –
blunt as bone, acerbic as our windfall apples.

The garden's overrun with teetering foxgloves, cigarette ends, soup tins,
broken televisions; luscious, hoary, interloping weeds.

A fat fox grazes the rubbish sacks. Cars lope, tacit, by the kerb.
I hold my breath in tightly and bless the motoring

wish, wish of my pulse. On TV, the newsreader speaks of riots. His voice
is muffled pips and swells – is someone underwater.

Animal Song (I)

Adults had sparse hair on their bodies,
except for thick shocks at the scalp,
          underarm, and pubic bone.

They measured, on average, 1.65 metres
tall. They walked steady on their
          hind legs, like startled bears.

They spent their lives on land,
          worked out their days to the sea's
                    slackening beat.

They were cossetted by stores
          of insulating body fat and by
scale-like or feather-like armour.

They hunted, insatiate, in packs.
   They huddled in groups, or hived
in pods of silicon, lime, and stone.

At night they covered their eyes to plumb
their own neural playback, experiment
          with impulse and response,
observe the shadow-play
                    of electrical storms.

At night they met to breed, dived –
subaqueous – inside each other's skins;
they choreographed aerobic dances.

Fossil remains of humanoid
          bodies discovered in East Africa
are 350,000 years old.

They apportioned *worth* – the value of
time, matter, or bodies – in terms
   of potential exchange.

They killed with an iron tool,
          a blow to the back of the head,
a mechanised procession/ poison,
          detonation, a slow
                    privation.

Prelude

(with electronica)

Already the weekend recedes into the distant distant distance.
In the kitchen's blue fog, Sunday's plates and glass rims bleed
spittle, our glamour remainders: fish bone, grits of mashed potato;
Rioja! Smuts of chocolate kisses! The living-room sofa is mournful (but
haloed with sunlight, morning's exposure spilling on into beatitude).
The sofa's haunted by the dint and notch of spines, our slumped arses;
the beating spectre of our voices. Outside, London revs and stammers in,
cranks out Monday. My earphone music keeps me heated in this earliness:
sirens and foliage phasing low on the soundscape. My footsteps' shuffle
hi-hats on the frosted kerb. The houses cough their callow squares
of window light, hug their angles close. My soundtrack veers me
from commute to noirish trek, from link road to film set; from slog
to mission, assignation, backlit by a grainy, mantling sky. An epic –
not a workday – engine powers the drive and drumbeat of my breath.
This swell and scratch is code, is the gutter and throb of pigeon wings;
they wheel and hike up, numinous, above the Old Street roundabout.

Lullaby Girl

(after Eileen McAuley's 'The Seduction')

flourbaby   doughbaby   squaresack   canvas
sewingmachinestitched   moonface/ no face
dumpy/ dinted   the sack sits tight   sweaty
against your polycotton   thin white shirt
chubby squat   school tie   long tail tucked in
against your chest

this is what
     it's like: heavysack   sleeps in a cardboard
box   under your bed   think back
to your doll   dad in the Argos queue
you wanted   water sloshed in its pink   belly
squeezed from between its pink legs   shaken
from blue   painted-on eyes   hinged lids   not
2lb flour bag in your skinny arms   you sing
hush hush in your head at the bus stop,   corner
shop

            could not bring yourself to look
last year   at Charlie Ward's newborn   pudgy
clay   animal   rumpled eyes   still
oblivious   in the pram though your classmates
crowded over its sky   made the right *oooo*
sound   in your head it was   animated   doll

you're still slight   gristle-breasted   nowhere
near woman   Miss Juegos said   *ask yourself:*
what care is needed by the flourbaby?   *who is*
with the flourbaby?   *where is the flourbaby?*
snug   in   the   bottom   drawer,   under
your magazines   *if there were boys at school*
you'd all be at it nonstop   Miss McClure says

limbsjumble/   snog   spittle   open
mouth never learning all   hunger and dumb-
ness

          Sian disappears takes her tight
belly   oval   swells   with her   Mr Wojcik
sings *Too Much Too Young*   over and over
you hear   Kelly, before her trial   is trying
for a baby

                    easy,   easy,   baby   a beautiful
shackle, or, like a ticket out   of somewhere,
maybe   rope ladder to cling to dig
fingernails in   something   *mine*   hot hot
shame and shameless/ bigbodied I   *made* this

in the first poem   you've studied in years
it's called *despicable*   this girl/mother-
hood state   called *feminine*   *void*

Iron Horse
[ahy-ern hawrs]

n (*pl* **iron horses**)

1. A mechanical stallion, mare or gelding. A contraption harnessing limb-work to whorl and feather spoke and wheel, engaging pedal and chain to centrifugal swing, streaking blue momentum. A wheel-blessed un-gulate built for crouch, for an arrowing of chin.

2. A hobby horse, un-tethered: steel-blue, or blue as quinine under UV will glow. I will pet and settle its aluminium spine. When my heels swivel, lift and engage – a point of departure.

3. A feat of balance – an act of pure will (*sl*). Wheezy-drunk, you cross the heath in a zigzag, tacking your bicycle-craft across the grassland. I keep you aloft and afloat and ballasted, singing *Molly Malone* in strict three-four time.

An aeroplane, tensing its whip-spun wheels from the runway, hangs like stopped breath.

Stray Dog

[strey dawg]

n (*pl* **stray dogs**)

    1. A tight-ribbed canid – its belly a skin drum.

In packs, they scrum through railings and wall cracks, in the wild state, slender-muzzled, ears cocked and noses honed to bolt. In alleys and silos, they snuffle for milk and meat. Though they're dry-nosed, their olfactory receptors brim: cacophonies of sweetbreads, cinnamon, piss-tang, petrol, shades of hops and turpentine – delirium.

    2. *Dog* is the root of his zen philosophy, he says. A dog only *is* and *does*.

Dog has no knotting gut, no slackening jaw at the price of fish, the fallout, our institutional implosions. Dog has no piquant sense of doom, but lives in simple verbs.

He wears his dog suit after work to watch the TV news. It's an all-in-one of teddy fur, sleek and moist with age, dabbed with tobacco and brown. He says *Our bodies are given life from the midst of nothingness*. I come home early, find him rootling through our bins – muzzle first, on all fours.

    3. Any street-sharp carnivore, any creature having canine teeth (*sl*); a flea-haven, haunter of parks, snarler of brute snarls, gleeful snouter of rumps. The stray dog melds with the harbouring dark, camouflaged as lamp post or wheel hub. He or she scarpers – slides under the night wind's silvered edge.

Enchantment

(backwards)

Before I can understand the words I watch my mother's fingernail trace inked
characters

– Again. Again. Her voice haunts every book.

A church spire tops the cake, our buttercream hill. Beyond
our garden fence, a forest I don't yet know is only three trees thick.

I spy beige lace, the dungy edge of my dress;
clammy salt of the flesh of my spindle legs. I breathe and breathe
the world's quiet, waiting for a God to speak.

She leaves the ward early: the stirrups, prim-cornered sheets, machine of shrieks.
She walks out, taking her body/ my new body with her.

Before I begin, the obstetrician leads a troupe of white-coated boys to her
bedside. They crane their goose-necks, jostle and hum. She's all *elderly*
primigravida, all belly – fleshy incubator, hands crabbed to the cradle of fluid
and skin; a miraculous, diagrammed cow, nosing her pain into the wool.

In gestation, she reads, *the woman ought to be careful of her diet, deportment, and*
exertions; mindful of her passenger and its soft little wants –

the swarm of digits demarcating, the body becoming,
indistinct as an aerial night-view.

(that musky print; the pages crumbed at the edges, like butter)

Here, she has fainted. He gently props her head against his foot and goes on
buying shelf brackets and spearmint paint. When she wakes, there's only the
shop counter's panelling and a thick slab of dust and sunlight. The floor's a
checkerboard pattern. Her belly is rude and hardboiled, glowering under the
tent of her dress.

Look! Out of nowhere, blossom erupts
over the patchy lawn. Wasps veer and crash.
A helicopter stitches the horizon.

Here I am making myself smaller: wren-small, bean-small.
I'm backing out of the room, backing out of the room, backing out of the room.

from **A General Dictionary of Magic**

Grizzly Bear
[griz-lee **bair**]

n (*pl* **grizzly bears**)

1. *Ursus arctos horribilis.* A large, North American brown; a wire-haired, silver-tipped, salmon-goading, spit-furred bear. Once widespread – now restricted.

2. A clumsy dance – part-zombie – in imitation of the tame, trained bear (*hist*); a dance to the side with a clunking, heavy step and little grace. The partners rear up, hands rigid and hooked as claws; an underworld song and dance, a degenerate act, a decided bending of the body that is wicked, scandalous, infamous and immoral, bawdy and obscene, corrupting the morals of the youth and public, eroding all civilised modes of taste and seemliness – and too filthy, obscene and immoral to be in decency further described. These days, everybody's doing it.

3. A constellation, you remind me. We're stalled at a comfort-stop, a lay-by outside Mapperton – the car's engine stewing gently, the sky a vapid darkness studded with white-hot plasma. And if it's a bear, it's a grizzly, silver-tipped. You say *Lots of people talk to animals. Not very many listen though.*

Footnotes to a Long-distance Telephone Call

> Where is the person speaking situated?
> PHILIP HORNE, 'Ford on the Phone'

---

1. I am calling from people like us and, of course, from girls like you.

I'm calling from the space we'll call 'my body': 5′9 and 144lb, beige skin, twenty-five teeth, short-sight in one eye (heritage: Nottinghamshire, Leicestershire, Stafford-shire, Norfolk, Taff Valley; shopkeeper, farm-hand, forester, gardener, prison officer, market trader, typist, scullery maid, cook, wife, teacher, lecturer, Londoner).

I am calling from lucky, lucky, lucky –
                 from the pillowy flake of butter croissants, and also
        from porridge with water and salt.

I'm calling from *when I was your age*, he says, *we washed our hair once a week*
        in a tin bath in front of the fire
             with coal tar soap.

2. I'm calling from boiled-egg and toast soldiers, tinned peaches in front of the gas fire, bottle-warmed sheets, indoor breath pluming –

wellies stomped then pulled off, just in out of the snow: brittle rubber, yellow salt; sweat from feet in three pairs of socks. Toes gone numb. The smell of something damp, medicinal, school cloakroom Savlon twang.

     I'm calling from paper aeroplanes, camphor boats, moth-traps and microscopes, lesson-plans, lecture-notes, marking fanned out on the living-room table

     and even, even, from '94, the beach at Mouettes, chocolate beignet in hand, about to head back to the sea's balmy, salt-blue slump.

3. I'm speaking, always, from lurched footing, from falling: on Bensham Road Kerry Wilson, fourteen, topples from her eight-inch platform heels and splatters down in the gutter. While she sobs and snots, mashed and red-faced, we push, shoulder and haul her up to her balancing act, onto those stilts. We haul her back to herself.

21

I'm calling from the careers woman smiles her best nurse smile for us and: *people think being a vet is just looking after cute animals but actually it's very, very difficult. Have you thought about, maybe, working as a receptionist?*

When I say I'd like to travel, the school careers software suggests *lorry driver*.
    Which is radical for girls in 1992, but I'm thinking more like *portrait painter, teacher, writer, writer*.

When Tanique and Michelle do amyl nitrate in double science, I think it's something they've made in a chemistry experiment. So many worlds, so many wonders. The boys at the youth club – bear hugs strong-arming our breasts, our breath.

I'm calling from the school art room, the sour dust of pencil shavings. Mr Wellerby's sketches of his best girls are pinned up like laundry: sharp chins, school ties, waterfall hair. Dirty, he called us girls when he left. Diseased.

4. Calling: see speaking aloud, my Radio 4 voice: *Just a Minute Gardener's Question Time* theme tune to *The Archers*. The sound of post-war. Sound of *well-spoken* and also *welfare-state*. Of people like people like us?

See also: muffled words, never-a-word. Because he doesn't like her to read (back before I am even a soot-speck or a single seed) gran buries her novels safe and deep in the laundry before he gets home: *The Big Sky, The Way West, The Ox-Bow Incident*. Cowboys; giant horizons.

I'm calling from nowhere but nowhere but the blank page: horizon, all the wild blue distance.

Well, yes, and, damson is its own pixel of sunlight
(she says, distracted) and when
you can no longer conjure up that odour –
petrol, sunscreen, sand – the damson fruit will spill
that old time's flavour, bring oil and plump
to your winded bones.

The Homecoming

(for Petrov Zalienko, the Hermit of Hendy Woods)

Hold your breath. Still yourself. Let no twig snap break the spell.
Stalk your way: slow tread of your soles' skin, iron
sweetness, moss and soil. Is this the way you remember it?
A heavy horizon; reeds skirting the water? Long-limbed
silhouettes of trees hone into keenness, into focus. Their fingertips
graze the canopy's quiet and dank: leafmould, woodsmoke.
You hear coots' grouching, low honks in the measly light.
Imagine bringing your dogs, your pigs if you had them, snouting
for tubers. Hoik yourself up into an oak's fat arms and survey
the land. Settle snug in the crook. You're invisible
again, your bones flush against the bark. All the king's horses
and all the king's men ride by in their pickups. Radios cackle;
headlights strobe the mulch into cranked up daylight. Later,
you'll scout for bilberries, cobnuts that rattle like broken teeth;
you'll whistle back at the herons' croaking, purse Tor grass
between your lips. Your hulk of a ship, the iron sea – gone now.
Blanks in time. Gunbarrel. Sallowface. Limpet-boy
balled in the rusty hull. What crisis? Here's a half shelter, lean-to.
Here's kettle smoke and a hearth. It's morning already. The embers
putter on. Your skin thickens, ossifies, gnarled as ash bark.
Your scalp's a muss of twigs. Your limbs? They could easily web
or grasp into roots. Your feet grow glossy and limber, drink
the underground mumble of fungi, carbon, hormones seeping like song.
Gulp this woodsmoke, leafmould, heavy horizon. Is this the way
you remember it? Reeds skirting the water, long-limbed? You're
home. No twig snap must break the spell so stalk your way, taste
moss, soil, your soles' raw skin. Still yourself; hold your breath.

from **A General Dictionary of Magic**

Wolf
[w*oo* lf]

n (pl. wulvz)

    1. Predator dog – canis lupus, mythical guzzler of grandma; gristly, yellow-eyed grand old dog of circumpolar distribution (formerly common); the thick-knit fur or hide of any such.

O, ghost-dog of us all: our shadow in slather and whelp – and what big teeth we have!

    (But for now, you're only twitching at the paws: snow-blind, deep under
        your sleep's shingle and tug.
    I think in your dream, you're seven again;
        your toes joggle crusted sand – the fat, greened shore).

    2. Also called: **wolf note** *Music*
A harshness or discord.

    (Your breath's a squeezebox crunch, a mewl.
    I watch for the retinal twitch, a reeling under your eyelids).

v

    3. To devour with rapacity.

(I have to tell you, while you're so attentive and rapt:

I have eaten the plums, the cloud-white loaf, the slices of ham, the hard-boiled eggs and all the shaved moons of sweetened, nut-spattered pastry; the soap of cold butter, the latkes, tomatoes and lima beans – which you were probably saving.

Careless, then, I split the carton and lapped up milk as it drooled and laked.
My thirst was a force so strong you'd glug saltwater to sate it, inhale great
lugs of drizzle; lick furring, days-old coffee dregs.

I drained the cupboards' undone cans – that greasy swill, that pudding slouch.
Like a picklock stray I scoffed and tore at wine, the gravy boat,
then, sighing, I sank my teeth into the sodden table's pulp and grain.

　　　All this gorged matter troubles and brims in my sleepless gut.
Now there's only this bed, your quietness and,
　　　　　outside, brazening light: forgive me).

To Read a History in the Earth

This deepest layer might, we imagine, be Proterezoic: a stratum of bacteria conserved in garden clay and builder's slate; see – the imprint of a child's tooth suspended in resin; here a fossilised pang of Vaporub, bath suds, the boozy wallop of milk.

> At the topmost of this stratum, a plastic toy telephone whose dial has been buckled by rain and screech laughter, depressed by prodding little thumbs. The dulled bell; metal on metal.

Some fifteen inches up: bluish limestone. Silt on silt compressed to cubist rubble. Here, the fossilised matter is more intact: a desiccated mosquito; a fern's total, balmy skeleton; a hamster corpse, a magnifying glass.

In this era the siblings discovered breath-holding, how the world rolls, dizzy, on its axis as you hug the earth after spinning on your heels. In the layers there are tinges of blood and dribble, taints of TCP.

In the concertinaed sediment: dissected tennis balls, and a crimped page of her favourite storybook: *the prince was quickly changed into a small, scaly dragon. What shall we do? said the queen.*

In the heights of this stratum: an unspooled VHS tape, empty tinnies, a packet of strawberry Angel Delight. In this time, the siblings avoided the garden's snarl of bramble and vetch grass, the augur of bonestink. The house loomed, ticking, at their backs. They clamoured, instead, on the kitchen steps.

And here, in the undershingle, we see a time when the children learned tactical absence and daysleep (the house that stood here had then become as eerie as a lone boot; its clockwork gripey and habitual). They grew tall, ferny spines and, nightly, roamed the map's blue contours, warming their hands on packets of chips and on cigarettes. Their voices hardened, tuned to the timbre of foxes' braying. They did not return to the garden.

And this, of course, is our topsoil (most of the stratum beneath was removed for forensic examination). But here we have feldspar, gin-bottle, fingernails, book ash; a soiled bootee.

Now that the turf is well settled over, there are only mossed dimples – the old foundations sketched in clover.

The house (its garden, the children, our history) has never been.

Anthropologies

She says it's haven't, not ent. Miz Jezameen Henacre wears long-tailed gloves
spilled over her skinnies like milk froth.

She fears palm-skin maybe, its thinness. She teaches me how to say her name,
sharpen the *een*.

She totters her bell skirts, her own self, here from the Mission house
mid-way through Sundays,

when our floor and walls are spanking and greased and the stove's brave
as new-forged kettle. See how we do.

Her voice is chipped pots and phonograph. A good clean place, she says.
She asks, and I tell her

how Jodie's gone last winter. She tuts and huffies at my sunrise starts,
the turnip and beet field,

my life as a plough horse. Only a half-ripe girl and my arms filling, hairing,
stubborn as bridge struts.

One Sunday, she asks why don't I think on marrying – I've enough years, just.
A married can settle at home with the pups

and just stew, keep home while he toils. I think on wifey Billie Navarre
and on my skipped-town sister, all sunup starts

and wash, wash, and harvest, all slog with kids in sling. I don't know this married
she speaks on. I sup my thick tea

and think on Luco McInnes last winter, the back room at the Victory hall.
Him, porter-thick and sweaty as licorice,

my coddled arse in his lap when he turned me, rocked himself inside, and me –
sore and happy like a seasoning dog.

She says I deport, I'd hire out well for wash, make a wife; I've a get-out. I say I can't leave the kidlets, dad and my cock-eye brother

a hand short in this dreggy winter. But a dreaming of wheat, a midday August softness plays in the mettle of my head.

Her voice is bell-hard, clappered as bells. In my cup of brew the leaves spin – sign of a hammer, maybe, a flit-gone gull.

Cloud; Silver Lining

(after W.S. Graham)

I hunch.
　　I fill: gathering muscle, breathing in water.
　　　　I pet the blue.
　　　I darken at sinister edges,
　　carry a cargo of rain.

　　　Beneath me, patched khaki and the birds' soot-speck swell
　　　　Beneath me, mops of dog
　　　　　tickle the surf, and the people
　　　are ambling down to the shrine of the sea.

　　　　Here I am, here I am again
　　　in the wet sand's glass –
　　my sky-tussocks, my flourishes.

Doomdark's Revenge

Doomdark leaks into the house
through a rotted angle of window frame.

The dusky scrape and hubble of him's
furred with a dandruff of gloss-white paint.

He draws in the ribs and sails of himself,
plants his manta ray body beneath

the settee and his one good eye rings out:
a peppered, indelible moon.

His claws *rasp* on the carpet's weave;
he squats, cold as cordite. While I am gone

he upsets the salt pot so that a sting
of crystals will slough my heels.

He gags sandy bile from his gut-depths,
coughs it in rivulets over the lino,

gnaws the furniture's edges and legs
to a snotty mash and draggle of fibres, peels

a nest of woodchip from the timber
of the kitchen door. Everything heaves, leans.

Dumb totem, he guards the back door,
still and implacable when I return.

I sit, sink. Doomdark clatters,
barks his low siren, cranks out blue sound:

a hounded, metallic whale. He springs, swipes
at the auricle of my ear with a scissor

of claw, then snaps back, jumpy as a ratter.
Now time's a stutter, a halt.

My fingers pinch at the bloody cartilage.
Oh the incessant intent of that one, good eye!

He sees, for all the house's bleach and clean,
my wrongs, tied up in brittle muslin

under my liver – a pocket of growths, of moulds –
the dank cheese of them resting inside me.

Home Economics

The road home spits words at us   drifts car honks and men's roars
like dandelion spores   like words that are slurred on all of their edges.
We look down. Look!   our skinny, beige legs   summer shorts.

Night's   forest, buckled tarmac   I walk our dog
around the empty park's perimeter fence.   Sometimes, slick cars skim
to a low halt; bass beats croon through pavement rifts.   The window
clicks, whirs   would I like to go for a ride?

Don't wear white if you want to look slim, Miss Collins says.   *Don't turn
   your back: when you close the door, when you enter a room.*

I'm   washboard, xylophone   not even beginning to dream
the itch and nub of new breasts.

You're too precious.   He swabs eraser over our exercise books
   terse cross-hatch   charcoal   Outside the science block
we see our teacher locked in a clinch with Tara Wilson.   She's leaning
back   like a filmstar.

On work experience, I wear my mother's clothes to the office.   Little skirts
lined with crackles of satiny static;   jackets that flail
from my coathanger shoulders.   I walk the carpet length to my desk:
low whistles and bleats. I look down. Look!
              Femur, shinbone, two proud kneecaps.

One minute I'm   washboard, spindle   not even beginning.
   The next? Nothing/   everything/   fits.

When I'm grown,   a boy I've long had a moony, cow–eye   desire for
will tell us all – Friday night, pub – about a film he's seen:
a man screams at his wife, he'll say.   The man tells his wife to cook him
some eggs.   He's drunk. *Make me some eggs, woman!*
The man slugs his woman in the face, and then he rapes her.   *Make me*
some eggs, woman! the boys will snicker,   sing.

The night   Claire's dad rolls home drunk and holds the bread knife to her
mother's throat, her mum says this: if he threatens her again in front
of the kids, she'll kill him. Next day, when he's gone,   she packs up
his things, takes them to his mother's.   She calls
the locksmith, changes the locks.

The school road home again. Across the street   boys chunter
out laughter. It's gravel rather than stones they throw.   Sting tickle
of cheekbone and collarbone. This is what passes for talking.

from **A General Dictionary of Magic**

Suckling Pig
[suhk-ling pig]

n (*pl* **suhk**-ling **pigs**)

1. A tenderfoot pig, thin-skinned and stupid with milk; scored and stuffed, blissing in the roasting tin as if only asleep next to the stove one whisky afternoon in January. Gelatinous, bird-hearted. Soft, still, unformed in the hooves and uncertain in the marrow [syn: *cochon de lait; lechon*]

2. A hog at the teat, elbowing in; at the pigpen gate.

Already it is difficult to say which is which: at the underground station, the strip-lit office cubicle, the screens' aqueous breath. Our anthro/porcine snouts nuzzle, muster in this crush. Not squealing but trotting sharply to the apportioned place, in the designated time frame.

3. Any artiodactyl animal of the hominid family, typically having a long-strung body, bristling skin, tail root itching under the sacrum.

You say: *they will use our hides for shields, our bones for tools, our bristles for brushes.*

What can I do but snort? What can I do but fatten on faux news ('Epic crocodile-shark death fight', 'Ten surprising signs of sleep lack') and shoe catalogues?

It's plain as a pig on a sofa just where we're headed –

O Woozle hunter, O righteous.

Shoplifter of the World

(after The Smiths' song 'Shoplifters of the World')

My first steal: an ice-pop, coaxed from the cornershop freezer: a brittle, syrupy limb that fused – beneath my shirtsleeve – onto my skin.

Second, a tidy slice of apple strudel (cadged behind the cafe proprietor's back). Its fudge of apples branded my pocket with a bloom of grease.

Years on, the shoes: size eight men's brogues. I had to have them, plied the storetags tenderly with my teeth. Their leather was needled with pattern, tracked like land. They slipped, like boats, beneath my feet.

And then, a child's bear with hammer-head ears; ten musky, gold-wrapped cigarettes; a book of dayglo paper that smelled of aspirin and lemon-water. Later, a rust-flecked penny-whistle; a pocket book of dirty jokes; a quart of value gin; an eight ounce rib eye steak.

Once, I filched a fold-out, paper diorama of my town at midnight, the blocks and structures picture-booked; on the glossy roof-tiles a cat lifted the whip of its spine.

Then, a five-foot rowan tree – tags on, uprooted – flat against my spine, its trunk aping my bones, its branches hunched into my sleeves; its feather and brush, its roots, hooking the loam of my feet.

Last, I stole a hatchling budgerigar who came, silent and willing, snug in the pocket of my winter coat. I taught her the basics of parroting: 'Roll out the Barrel' and 'Whisky in the Jar' and *Not to worry! Not to worry!*

Fawn

What's left of the fawn is impressionistic and a little broken:
her dark eye batting improbable lashes; a light stink

of piss and mothballs; night-vision, the dry scour of her tongue,
a hoof-print at the door-jamb. Fawn lived on air

and pure sunlight. She would not suffer the body's humiliations:
its bleating, animal muscle, the MEAT of us all.

Her skin slunk, bone-tight and wheaten, a spanking new drum.
Each night she dreamed soft, as if flumped

on a pillow of marshmallow arms, but woke to her rickety
fawn body, rusty and clanged

as an abandoned zoo. Nobody wanted to look at her. On the bus
into town her skirt gaped, disclosed

the clenched, moon-white of her kneecap, her Bambi calfbone.
Only the engine spoke, and spoke.

Opposite, a stranger-woman's eyes mumbled and spilled salt-water.
How can a body carry it: this hunger; such myopia?

Poem in Which I Consider My Labours

It's like the cotton mills of the eighteenth century,
he says. Yes – yes. My mouth

is open and tilted, a golf hole. Outside, the students
squall, butting their foreheads

against the dome of the afternoon. I am stunted,
frayed from the defibrillator kick

of early wakeups, shifts that begin in dim morning toffee
and end in the dumb blackout of sleep.

Yes – I'm deafened by the machine's gut-snap clatter.
Such heat and dust! Such grotesque accidents!

The walls are shored up with staples and knucklebone.
I pack thick wads of student assignments

(my students – that puddle of yellow beaks) into my bag,
and set out into the dark

where my ancestors stand in a wonky, makeshift chorus.
They're hard-fired, lean as striplings,

got up in their double-darned best. Their sighing's
the engine of my endeavour;

their sighing's the bright sting of my luck,
and ADULT is all about using your anger

just so: kitten piston, slow combustor,
mechanism of the soft intestine.

from A General Dictionary of Magic

Scanderoon
[scan-der *oo*n]

n

A leather drinking pouch suspended from a cavalry officer's belt. 1863: *If a man may rest, he might quaff the dregs of his scanderoon.*

Or, scanderoon: a rainy day stash: If a woman may finally rest, she might break out her put-by scanderoon. She might eat up every last salted crumb and hike off into her sleep

> the hills demarcating – finding focus
> > as we taxi down from altitude; the canopy's deepening greenness.

Or, scanderoon: a homing pigeon, supposedly of Persian origin, of a breed having long heads, bodies, and legs, broad shoulders, and a long iron-clad compass bill with moderate wattle. A slick, swerving bird.

Or, the message a pigeon carries around its neck through thousands of miles – in war, or peacetime. Untraceable, off-web, hidden up there inside fat cloud or behind a brush of sun.

Or scanderoon (*hist*): in Rev James Stromingam's *Whitby Glossary*, 1791: 'Scanderoon: a popular mis-quote; a sentence or phrase wrongly apportioned.'

For instance, I never called my dictionary 'prison';
I never doused it in bleach or buried it, never said 'If I can't dance, it's not my dictionary.'

When all the rivers are breached and the lodestars dark;
when the sea re-hems the map
and your bones are long gone cold;

when the right word is as rare
as a snowbird in hell – I'll still be circling in,
trusting my magnet-beak, striking for home.

Catalogue of Strange Fish

From the unfathomed, farthest away from the light, from the sea's
iron guardedness they come –

pin-eyed, with flesh like tree bark. Their jaws are gorgeously spiked,
ragged with toothpick teeth, goon teeth, prison bar teeth.

O anglerfish, vampire fish, oarfish, goonch. A strange fish holds himself
upright and fast to the park railings. He is white knuckled.

His eyes focus upwards as if counting or reciting, tugging at the brain's
stubborn pinions. When you ask if there's somewhere

he needs to get to, he only sets his jaw harder. You both know that if he
acknowledges you, he'll fall. Every one of your dreams

is about the president, however tangentially. Each morning, pre-waking,
mucid insects seem to attach themselves

to your collarbone and gnaw in at the marrow. What if we could all say
whatever came first to mind, whenever we wanted to? No

perusal. *Scullion! Arse-wipe! Warp-faced pignut!* Invincible as a body
that's snug in the womb. What if we could all get

whatever we wanted, whenever – as in the fairy tale? On the beach
at Marazion the surf is spangled with mackerel scales.

The sands heave with stranded bodies, silver bullets drying
and curling up in the winter light, so close to home.

from **THE BLOWN DEFINITIONS**

There are places we fear, places we dream, places whose exiles
we became and never learned it until, sometimes, too late.

THOMAS PYNCHON

In the year 2068 or thereabouts Gil Laundacht's island home, Ilha de Piñeiros, is fast becoming uninhabitable. Ilha de Piñeiros is a former colonial territory where the indigenous language, Maphachti, is dying out and almost all of the people have emigrated to the mainland. Through conversations with his English granddaughter, Rosa Huse, and through his radio show, *Voz de Piñeiros*, Gil explores his past and attempts to keep the language and culture of his homeland alive.

VOICES:

GIL LANDAUCHT: a former journalist and an inhabitant of Ilha de Piñeiros.

ROSA HUSE: Gil's granddaughter, a secondary school teacher living in South-East England.

PIOTR DAMINE: Rosa's partner, a metropolitan housing engineer.

LUCIA CARDOSO *(deceased)*: a software developer and Gil's ex-partner. Luisa is the mother of Rosa's father, Ruben.

LISEL CAREVAS: an expert on the work of poet Claude Mesito, a well-known poet from Ilha de Piñeiros.

DAVID ANTEUS: the island's archivist.

WEATHER FORECAST CHORUS: All voices except the dictionary.

DICTIONARY: An electronic dictionary voice, halfway between robotic and human.

I: Claude Mesito

GIL *(radio voice):*
Lup Tolernos and his Violent Orchestra there. It's six thirty this glorious
Wednesday evening. Greetings, bem-vindo

and *kaino* to all of you out there. It's been a boozy, breeze-scuffed day
here on the ilha. The pine trees

are spilling out that curious, cough medicine scent. So, as you slink yourselves
home, in the last of the light,

it's time for some ilha tales from Lisel Carevas. Today, we're shooting the breeze
about our esteemed friend, our island poet, Mister Claude Mesito.

LISEL:
Thank you, Gil. Well of course there's no shortage
of stories about Mesito – o malandro velho.

I'll begin with only flat-out what I know,
and omit all rumour and gossip...

Claude Mesito was a fisherman.
His boots were patched with tar;
he whistled birdsong under his breath.

On Sundays in summer he'd sleep on the front porch,
flat out, jaw lolling open –

GIL:
Remember that monstrous beast of a cat that slept on his chest?

LISEL:
Lolo, yes. That thick blanket of cat, even in summer...

Mesito was a quiet one. He hardly spoke, except
to buy his newspaper and groceries –

GIL:
Which means there were stories galore about him.

Once, when my father was five years old or so, for a dare,
he sneaked into Mesito's one room hut.

(Sound of children chattering, laughing.)

Dad only stood beyond the beech wood door
for three, tight, breaths, but afterwards he claimed to know Mesito's secrets.

GIL'S FATHER (BOY 1):
At night, he sleeps in a big tin bath.

GIRL:
He makes weird tisanes and potions at night:
fish-blood and witching herbs. If you get too close, he'll turn you into a –

GIL'S FATHER (BOY 1):
He eats cat food out of a tin! I saw him.

GIL:
He'd boil you up for dinner if you got too close, we said;
he'd use your skin for new boots, your hair for fishing nets.

LISEL:
Those were the popular legends, yes.

I remember Claude as bloodshot, but strong-toothed.
He went out, oilskin buttoned to his chin,
every day except his rest-day, observing the sea
as if it were a giant cow he tended to.

(The sea, gulls.)

At four am, when the island was hush-hush and the sky
still licorice, he'd tumble down to the jetty and set out.
His catch was tuna, shrimp-fish, monkfish, yellow crab.

GIL:
He sold it?

LISEL:
To the cafés and restaurants as far as I know, here and on the mainland.
Households, too.

He conversed, occasionally,
with Mala at the grocery store, about the cricket –
matches he'd picked up on his giant, leather-jacketed radio.

(Sea / white noise sound fading in.)

No one had known Mesito's father and they said his mother
was an outlander. She'd appeared on the sands one day,
half-cut and sea-draggled, regarding her own, distended belly
as if astonished by the sudden imposition.

She offered it up in her hard, brown hands.

GIL:
Growing up, I thought of Mesito as part of the weather. Always –

LISEL:
Looming, I suppose – yes. Hands in pockets.
He hung – like sea-mist – about the corners of the island.

But he was content, I'd like to think: a steady, winter snail.

One fall, we hadn't seen him for at least a week.

GIL *(Overlapping)*:
It was my uncle Theodor who found him, face down in the bunk...

LISEL:
His flesh was already sunken, but so pickled with salt and fish guts
there was no other scent.

GIL:
A heart attack.

LISEL:
That's what the doctor said.

It was the grocer, Mala, afterwards – sweeping and airing the room
to keep Mesito's soul comfortable – who found the poems.

GIL:
The notebooks.

LISEL:
Mmm – in the bread bin. Lacy with age and larvae, spiral bound, the *Silvine* brand.

Mala sat cross-legged on the floor and read each one:
that sooty, schoolboy text. The island was there in those pages, in squared,
biro handwriting: all its crags and curiosities.

GIL:
And the poems? Can you tell us more?

LISEL:
As it stands, we have only what was found in Mesito's house that day.
All in Maphachti – no Portuguese, no English.

After the first discovery, there were other 'discoveries' of his work –
but they were all found to be fabricated.

GIL:
Could you, perhaps, read us something of Mesito's?

LISEL:
I'm going to read number seventy-two, which is untitled, from the first folio:

In translation, of course, from the Maphachti:

(Sea sound fading in.)

Over my little boat, the clouds go reeling.
They're cauterised with fire, like the saints in church windows!

Cold air coughs in my windpipe; fish
weave intrigues of shadow. They sluice by, gawp
at my planetary face – its creases and canals.
What do you think of, fish, in your shale valleys and gulleys?

This morning I think of saying to hell
with all of this business, swimming out into air
as viscous and giving as water. All of us:
Mala, Pepito, the boys at the cliff-end,
lifting our feet up, flippering out.

II: Sleep Psalm/ Weather

ROSA *(interior voice)*:
O for the neurotransmitter flip, mind's hauling anchor,
a quick skidding into sleep's slipstream –
night's warp of pebble and water.

I don't want to dream in the day's steamrollered syntax.
Here's to my night language: here's to cartoon werewolves
re-enacting our most toxic rows in mime.

My bedsheets turn and buff to bleached bone, ivory;
day's trash is shunted
and ploughed clear of the causeway.

WEATHER FORECAST CHORUS:
Moving on to the East Atlantic landmass and surrounding islands:

In the early hours from two am, we can see
an intense area of low pressure starting to spiral rapidly towards the continent,
hitting the west coast with rising winds, successive banks of heavy rain.

ROSA:
Some disturbance of sleep; some damage to fences and unhoused livestock.

WEATHER FORECAST CHORUS:
From three a.m. we can expect to see:

Strong currents, pounding their hooves on the ocean's bedrock.

(Galloping horses crescendo.)

And in the atmosphere: great lugs of sand and muck; loose plankton,
shoals of great white shark and, above them, migrating geese blown off course,
and scrags of polythene –

like kites, like albatrosses.

LUCIA:
At night Rosa is startled, every now and then, by sirens.

(Horse hooves thunder.)

ROSA *(groggily)*:
What if it's a hurricane lockdown? Another bomb alert?

PIOTR:
Go to sleep, love. It's nothing – miles away.

(Hooves thunder continues; a clock ticks in the foreground.)

ROSA *(sighing)*:
Not tickering budget spreadsheets nor colour-zoned schedules.
Never forensic, frieze-frame re-runs of the imbecilic things
I've done or said –

LUCIA:
Not fear's erosion, its glacier tracks.

ROSA:
Not his prone body and not its absence – the pillow
pummelled, becoming flesh – flour baby,
featureless.

Maybe, then, I'll imagine Shapwick's moonlit silos;
not sirens but owlsong, the loam exhaling, wheat
cut, shocked – safely gathered.

WEATHER FORECAST CHRORUS
The wind: a whimper, now rising to gale force seven
the wind, herding vast bisons of cloud across the badlands of the sky.

The air, like flint sparking; like a fist connecting with jawbone.
The gulls, braying like dogs.

LUCIA:
As the ice on the Arctic surface melts away, the less
there is the less there is. A feedback loop is a feedback loop

but the white-flowered, sour-tasting wood sorrel blooms, and the
elderflower blossoms glow, and the fields purr and the frosts fall back
and the winds lean the building so its girders pulse a belly-drone.

ROSA *(shifting)*:
I shore myself against the boulder of his spine.

LUCIA:
So she ploughs on, towards her sleep's dumb heaviness.
Outside, the buildings are silver with pixel-light;
their cracked paint's damp with night-sweats.

Some nights, she shifts the kitchen vent panel free of its teeth.
She climbs up, shivers her body into the cooling tunnel then

(Dull sound of clanging metal.)

up, to the roof.

(Digital ringtone music; low babble of voices.)

ROSA:
The megacity stews in its juices, like a giant puddle of pin-light:
call centres, offices wired for other time zones –
the smog of night voices.

LUCIA:
The tarmac oozes heat, and the soles of Rosa's feet roast and thicken, or soften
in the yellow dregs of rain.

(Winds, low creaking of girders.)

On storm-nights, curled like a bean
in their bed, eyes clamped shut, she almost sees her rooftop eyeline –

ROSA:
The rain, walling down, grey as the estuary, pissing down from an oily cloudburst.

LUCIA:
Winds leans the building so its girders sing.

(Girders droning – low sounds and harmonics.)

Winds etch new, wraith-harmonics into her sleep.

WEATHER FORECAST CHORUS:
Tonight's storm won't bring the record surges we saw last month
but defences are liable to be breached.

Citizens are advised to remain in secure, bonded lock-down
until 09.45 tomorrow, standard time.

ROSA:
O sleep-reel, shadowplay, celluloid fiend, your jittery dance
snagged on repeat. O forty winks –
knockout veer into glamour and dark,

to bloom my lungs with that valley weather – drowse
and green cut with river water – might be enough
to sustain me through any misfortune, any windfall.

III: Some Definitions

DICTIONARY:
Off-limits
Noun

    1. An edge land; a barren, wasted land.

ROSA:
Not necessarily wasted. Or barren. Just somewhere that used to be lived in but isn't.

DICTIONARY *(overlapping)*:

    Where the earth holds itself sloppy as mouldered leather; a shrunken
    sprawl of abandoned hulks – brick-box buildings on shallow soil; any
    (pre-lived) floodplain hinterland speckled with scrub and brush.

GIL:
A floodplain then?

ROSA:
Most often. The word can be used to mean naff, too: a bit beyond the pale.

DICTIONARY:

    2. An area lacking something: *Culturally, the town was an off-limits.*

    3. A depository for lost things: blossoms of polythene, polypropylene,
    tendrils of yellow piping.

ROSA:
Dumbbells, fridges, blister packs, six-packs, empty tinnies…

What next? A Maphachti word?

GIL *(slowly)*:
Em'kator

DICTIONARY:
Noun

    1. A particular species of long-winged, passerine bird with reddish wingtips
    (as if paprika-dusted), noted for its migratory habits; a bird with a cry
    like an urgent, gargling macaw.

GIL:

More like a cockatoo than a macaw, I'd say. And Em'kator isn't only a bird. It's also a person: one who leaves and returns, leaves and returns to the ilha several times – like a yoyo, caught up in its own momentum.

DICTIONARY:

     2. A flibbertigibbet; a turncoat; one who flits between places, cultures, decisions; one who cannot make up her or his mind between cities –

GIL:

Lovers –

DICTIONARY:

Butter or margarine; fried or scrambled eggs.

GIL:

An em'kator – in the past, at least – would always come back, would breathe the muggy, salt and pine-sap air as the ilha ferry docked, or as the aeroplane door slid open,

and find, in that dusty, fishbone earth, some vital molecule, some chemistry that made the place, despite everything, irresistible.

ROSA:

Another one?

GIL *(overlapping)*:

OK. Something different. A bit more functional.

I know…
(slowly)
Marooat

DICTIONARY:

Adverb

     1. A negative – used to indicate stubborn denial or dissent; not at all, in any degree or possible circumstance, not by any means.

GIL:

From the Maro – the ilha's long-dead, tight-lipped volcano that grouches over the land.

DICTIONARY:
It means no, essentially.

GIL:
It means, most often, never – and you have no right to ask.

ROSA:
Another? Something rarer, maybe.

GIL:
Rare? Let me think.
OK, here goes:

(slowly)
Ke'toon

DICTIONARY:
Noun
> 1. A particular time of the year, a week or two after the first buds of the
>   rainy season.

GIL:
Not just the time of year. Not exactly by the calendar, I mean.
It's also to do with weather patterns and the cycles of the moon. What you get is:

dry bottled heat, then piddly thunderstorms, then deep, massaging sun, then
apocalyptic downpour…

(Rain, and birdsong, fading in.)

DICTIONARY:
Heavy precipitation.

GIL:
Apocalyptic downpour.

DICTIONARY:
Have it your way then: downpour – until the island is running with muddy veins,
the coffee fields and groves spangled with papery blossom, the porch-fronts blaring
out purple rosebay and papelillo, all of nature pumped with adrenaline, verdant,
dancing a bad, drunken uncle dance with itself.

LUCIA *(interior voice)*:
Until, back then, the hibiscus and azaleas threatened to overwhelm us with
their sickly blossom, fronding leaf and suco, and we retreated indoors, a little
high on oxygen and pollen.

GIL:
Legend has it that traditionally all of the children
on Ilha de Piñeiros were conceived in ke'toon.

ROSA:
Can I access the dictionary?

GIL:
Any time you like. And it's a fascinating read.
But all that's there, these days, is —

ROSA:
Memory?

LUCIA *(interior voice)*:
Absence and forgetting;
the distinct outline of our vanishing.

IV: An Ilha Tale

GIL *(radio voice)*:
It's five fifteen and I'm here out on the Maro, with our dispenser of ilha wisdom, archivist David Anteus.

David: we were talking, yesterday, about the ilha's sacred – or *paunit* – places. We're going to talk, today, about one of our sweetwater places, *N'bal sir* or 'sweating rock'.

DAVID ANTEUS:
Thank you, Gil. Yes.
So, as we've said, this was – according to the myths – the very first spring on the ilha, the water that brought life and liveliness to this hulk of volcanic rock.

GIL:
These days, of course, it's full of seawater more often than not.

DAVID ANTEUS:
Yes –
But for a long time the pool was absolutely sacrosanct. There are many stories about this rock, and the spring. The one I'm going to tell is pretty recent, actually. But we know it incorporates earlier tales.
I must have heard this version from my cousin...

GIL:
Great. Go ahead, David.

DAVID ANTEUS:
So –
One dry summer, a mainland city woman stays
on the island, alone with her child in a house at the edge of the village.

A hydro corp accident's done for her little girl's father;
his strong lungs have starved of air until

they've quietly imploded. Things aren't easy for the woman: mourning
his body, picturing his hands at the lock each time night rattles the shutters....

The ilha's weird geographies remind her of the child's father.
The islanders show her kindnesses,

57

reveal their idiosyncrasy, some secrets:
the wild zones; where the best coffee berries grow; places

for swimming on sun-blenched days; wild garlic to eat
and, of course, fish.

KELL *(interior voice)*:
Sardines, mackerel, perch –

DAVID ANTEUS:
There is one place, though –

(Slow splashing of water, birdsong.)

on a blue hillside just beyond what used to be the village, where the water
pools, snow-cold and almost unnaturally limpid, like buffed aspic–

where locals rarely fish, or swim. This, despite
the perch swimming beneath the weeds.

KELL:
It's sacred – I've heard.

DAVID ANTEUS:
While local teenagers might once have lounged and littered
in the island's other waterways, this place remains
undisturbed, even by breezes.

KELL:
The water, they say, comes from an ancient spring,
This is where the island's mosses, pine trees and green hills first burst forth.

DAVID ANTEUS:
Although, to the objective eye, the pool looks
as if it might be filled by crag-caught, trickledown rainfall.

LOCAL 1:
It's a cure for sickness: fevers, rashes, liverache –

LOCAL 2:
Don't know about that. Wouldn't go near it if I were you.
Don't touch, I was told –

DAVID ANTEUS:
If the pool is disturbed by one iota, one story goes,
the spirits that bless the spring might take offence and hide
beneath the earth's mantle forever, leaving the island stark and bald.

(Pause.)

One Saturday afternoon, at the very height of summer, when her girl
is barely a year old, the woman takes her child on a walk in the hills.

(Baby babbling, birdsong and trees.)

Rounding a corner, she comes to a rough set of steps cut out of thick turf,
leading down to a scraggy, rock-strewn pool.

LUCIA *(interior voice)*:
She sees, at once, that this is the mythical place described in the bar-tales.

DAVID ANTEUS:
Rushes and bladderwort strain up and away from the water.
Her own reflection (bundled,

with the child on her back) looms, sharp in the pool.
The sun hangs thick in the sky, a heavy coin branded onto the haze.

KELL *(as if talking to the baby, calming)*:
You lie down here in the grass here.
I don't believe those stories – do you? Water is water.
It looks so cool…

DAVID ANTEUS:
Kneeling, with the child in the juicy grass beside her,
the woman bends forward and gently cups a palm into the water.

The shock of cold numbs her finger-joints, but the water is sleek and downy.

(Splashing sound of water being scooped up and drunk.)

The taste is mossy, and there's something else – a metallic edge. She lowers
her face.

LUCIA *(interior voice)*:
She notes the glassy meteor of her own dark, reflected eye –

DAVID ANTEUS:
And continues to splash, to drink. Bone-white, tiddler fish flash amongst the rocks; baby snuffles, contented on the grass.

Sweat courses and pools in the small of the woman's back; the water soothes her gullet –

LUCIA:
Like iced honey.

She strips off her T-shirt, bra, cut-offs and knickers, sloughs off her sandals and plops her feet, step by step, into the softness of the water.

(Wading / water sound.)

The rocks drop sheerly away beneath her; the pool is deep – up to her chest in a few, small shuffles. Her toes stir humus and algae in the shingle.

The water mutes her skin to pudgy amber.

(Sharp intake of breath, then muffled, underwater.)

She crouches her knees, draws her head down underwater.

(Drumbeat / heartbeat, getting louder.)

LUCIA *(interior voice)*:
For all her ears' silence and bellow she only hears the rough beating of her own heart, brimming over a cramped cage of bones.

KELL *(interior voice)*:
Next thing, I think I hear –

(Baby crying, as if from underwater.)

LUCIA:
The baby, just woken.

DAVID ANTEUS:
She kicks her legs, and her body powers upward, as if one,
sinewy mass of brawn. She can't feel her toes –

LUCIA:
They must be numbed...

DAVID ANTEUS:
Pushing her shoulders up, she surfaces.

(Heartbeat, louder.
Gasping sound, as if desperate for air.
Baby squawking, full-throated.)

The woman launches her body towards shore, flailing on the slippy rock.

It's OK, she says, but her voice, as she hears it, is all wrong – fat and gravelled
as if the pond's murk churned and clogged in her larynx. *It's OK lovely*, she says –

(White noise shifting to low-pitched porpoise sound).

LUCIA *(interior voice)*:
But the consonants are barely audible; her vowels gripe and groan
like the last throes of a broken accordion.

DAVID ANTEUS:
She flaps her tired arms but can't grasp the overhanging slates or branches.
The water's stone-cold now, and tight, banded around her lungs.

She hears herself cry out, and the sound is strange: lone and heavy
as a gull moping at the fisheries.

(Porpoise sounds.)

The small boy who comes, in the early evening, attracted by the baby's
whimper, finds the pool disturbed by a large, dark-eyed porpoise,
its whiskers honed, like antennae towards the cawing of the baby.

GIL:
And, not knowing what else to do, the boy toddles
the hungry child towards its honking mother, down in the water.

DAVID ANTEUS:
And when darkness falls –

DAVID ANTEUS / GIL:
The villagers haul mother and pup away to the godless sea.

(The sea, gulls.)

V: From the first quarto of Claude Mesito

(in translation from the original Maphachti)

No. 15

N'Whaldu

Leagues below, on night's seabed
you come – solemn, like molasses –
through sleepy homesteads,

bare-ankled, towards me. The sky
is the sky is the sky is the skin
of the night. I inhale your spirit, bitter

like a tin-cup of burnt coffee.
You sit in the green of my belly, hear
my blood hum its gospel, slow.

I can't speak. I will speak to the notch
and leather of your elbow, your scarred
knee. I will bring you a glass of water.

No. 73

Under your inexorable discipline

I want to know everything, be it ever so unfortunate:

tell me about waking up scorch-mouthed, as dawn bears in.
In your dream, you were doing something wrong:
stealing a bird's egg, eating
the last pancake, telling a lie.

Tell me about the geese, how they *whurrup*
and coast, cranking out their greyscale wings.
You say the afternoon coffee is pissweak
and reminds you of singed hair.

Here, in the lightning's galvanising
dalliance, in its flickering branch and filament –
short-circuiting the bloating sea –
I will espouse your curious electricity:

The shark-pout of your mouth as it troubles
mine; your brilliantine voice
edging towards sighing.

There's riptide in my belly as you eat
your sandwich, shovelling, thoughtless
as an eight-year-old boy. Meantime,
surprisingly, our blood still circuits.

POSTSCRIPT

Día de los Muertos

Only the dead have seen the end of the war.
PLATO

My guests are insubstantial as horizon clouds, tetching and blinking
themselves towards visibility. They're like toddlers: bleary and milk-sour after napping.

I've decorated every surface of the room with their curling photographs, their cold
poses – captured eyes. I've stewed tea, sliced pink salmon sandwiches

from softest, cloud-white bread. I invite them to sit – my holograms, my dusty, gone
beloveds, whose heels hover stubbornly, inches over the vinyl flooring.

Lily-Rose strides to the window, surveys our late roses and the battalion
of cars that have settled now, nose to tail, by the street. She drips ash; she's tangy, downy

with cold cream and cigarettes. And granddad's hard as mica –
a wheezing rook in the TV corner, terse and muscled, almost fossil. He won't speak,

but *kaahs*, his hat tipped over his nose. My other granddad is already off
in the backyard scrub, clearing the brambles, planting, letting his brown hands, his brown

mind, clear and blanken in the bracken and loam. I balance my cup of sweet tea,
the rhythm of chink and hush, the scrape of saucers. Beside me Charley and Marguerite

soak up the garden view: *Isn't the weather beautiful?* I say. *Isn't this grand?*
and *how have you been?* Caitlin is outside nursing a whisky mac, studding the lawn

with her spiky heels, teasing next door's roaring cat
with her gangly, see-through limbs. I want to ask them what it's like: to be only pixel

and decayed particle, only an actor in all our imaginings.
But, of course, they're pulse-less and placeless: diffuse, distributed, even in the moon's

gurning face, in the grinding of bus gears, the first-light rustle of parakeets.
Charley throbs out his greenish, beatific light, takes another slice of almond cake.

And Inga turns to me, shrugs her wan self out. There's smiling inside
her distant, radio voice, and she speaks without moving her lips: *Well*, she says,

                    you never expected this to be easy – did you?

Pistons and Bones

I remember my mother explaining very practically
how she thought shock therapy worked:
electric current recalibrating the skewed chemistry of the brain.
I sat in the back garden and imagined electrons like vitamin C powder
in a sphere of water, fizzing into an orange flush.

In one of the photographs, my grandfather's skin is pillowy and buoyant.
He is twelve years old, gaze turned inwards, standing next to his brothers
who are stiff in their well-worn army uniforms.
In the other photograph, he is herculean and broad-chested –
His suit struggles to contain him; my mother is getting married.

    He was never got right by the old regimes. He was never
    got right by the shared clothes, the Gideon bible.
    Most visitors regarded him, he said, way a cow would look at you.

On a bad day, my mother said, her father would calmly announce after dinner
that he was going to stand in the road and wait for something to run him over.

On a bad day, she said, he would bolt out of the house and away,
taking his clothes off as he went and leaving little fabric puddles in his wake.
His children would run out, scooping up those familiar garments and forging
                                            on after him.

    On a bad day, my mother said, he would bolt out of the house and away.

Was it freedom, to loose himself first from his house and then
from his jacket, shirt and shoes, sloughing himself out of his everyday life?

    I have sometimes imagined him keeping going,
    peeling off his pale, broad, Nottingham skin to dump it lightly in the gutter.

        And then the knots of his muscles;
        and then the twiggish veins, his pistons and bones.
        And then his pulse – the ghost of all this momentum – hovering inert
        like a jellyfish, before expiring into the Tuesday morning air.

Wayfarer

(for Willow)

Though I'm a dog-eared page, and tired, and the day stank, I'll sing your lullaby.
I'll lift up the croak and rattle of my voice to bring your lullaby.

Although you don't need a voice, these days, to find your wooded sleep,
you ask – so here's a basket of rushes, mossy bank, a wayfinder string: your lullaby.

Beyond your window trees gripe, winded, and the air glowers gunmetal,
while sparrows fret and the sky creaks shut its velvet hinge, I spin your lullaby.

Strong as my body, sure as true North, this *hush little, rock-a-bye.*
Though storms may burn, glaciers rip and the cold rain lash and sting: your lullaby.

This room's an ark of amber light, plush animals, plastic gimcrack, fidget
of milk-tooth thread. Breathe melody's current, the watery tug and swing, your lullaby.

Shuck off the day's brass band and Kodachrome, the BPM, your monkey-jig;
let sleep tarry your mind's machine – every cog of it, every pin, your lullaby.

Let my song, then, Kate's voice-forged rowing boat, or cradle – or loaded gun –
keep you, carry you, safe to sleep's threshold and far, far on: your lullaby.

When Glamorous Women Make Age-appropriate Dressing Statements

(for Alison Winch)

When I turned 40 I became my father. He'd lean in, wrinkle
his forehead. Or cock his head like a curious dog.

No pressure, then, to go clubbing at 10p.m. or stay out
drinking till dawn. I'd tamed the inner critic in my head – the one

with the cattle-prod, the catapelta. I can still drink alcohol
until it flows from my eye sockets. My head careens and my hangovers

are biblical. I refuse to buy anything that needs dry cleaning
or even ironing. These days, bossy is 'gets shit done'.

Shy is a good listener. It's all about how you use it. I wonder now if I'm
less Carrie Bradshaw, more Su Pollard. I cry often:

at game show wins, song lyrics, the milky slump of a child's
dropped ice-cream cone. Now 'no' is a complete sentence

and the unwashed look is always a runner. The experts say:
wear silver shoes. Or gold. Just a bit of ooh and not quite

so boring then. The experts say: *LAPD. Bono. Billy Idol...*
these are all looks to avoid. As is Tony Blair, in some very hot

countries, wearing white linen. Death has become a preoccupation.
This is in some ways a positive thing. There's still time

to think, experiment, fail brilliantly. There is always a plan B
(which doesn't mean boozing till I get the blues. This

is *my* weekend). The experts say: *avoid pie-crust collars.*
Hair bows. Bows on shoes. Anything Di would have worn, niet.

Perk it up. Splashy earrings. Popcorn highlights. What is
the opposite of perk? The narrow road to the deep north.

Which is actually liberating (and oh-so-wise). I'm no longer afflicted
with the blind optimism of youth. But I can still

laugh at myself. Dance like it's Snapchat. Rock my own style.
It's my weekend: I'll take it, take it.

California

After seven years' holiday-less, I'm scarred, like this land, with ghost rivulets,
hardened against the liquid shock – voluptuous

time, lard and vein of it splayed out like a coast road, forest road, a slick of freeway
falling away beneath the bus wheels,

like the green bay lurching towards us as we land. At immigration, the officer asks
Do you have ten thousand dollars? and I can't

quell a seal's bark laugh. *Are you OK ma'am?* Deeply, as is my inconvenient sense
of humour. *It's not about what*

you deserve is maybe the best piece of wisdom my mother gave me, which means
the cotton-ball fog peeling away

at the horizon's tacky, cornflower edges; the heat blooming, pouring in now
from our toes up to our ears,

our stunned scalps – a transfusion, or some new rite of spring – as we drive away
from the city: all this is ludicrous glut; boundless, bottomless margarita.

Animal Song (II)

The rarer they get, the fewer meanings animals can have.
Eventually rarity is all they are made of.

HELEN MACDONALD

I shuffle my sitbones back   neck craned
like a turtle's towards   the dashboard

where my fingernails
          flutter a rainpulse.   I scan
   the windowscreen horizon, scan my eye
corners for
     a breath-catch twitch, a familiar startle:

rabbitfur, gullwing, pheasant russet or
   crest – ear – escaping rear – the fractured
animal parts we still glimpsed (though
a rarity) when we were kids;

these days we encounter those same beasts
in glassy hallucination, wishful
          mindtricks   or soupy, in dreams.

Those bodies of bone/fur/flesh/ were,
together, our compass   their chitter
and call   a conglomerate pattern
of sound we set, and knew, our song by. Not

this blankened land, no other mind for miles.

Lunchtimes we spill/stalk down from
     our concrete warrens, eat paper cupfuls
     of mossy, green-specked chaw.
The advertisements
               promise pureorganicnatural.

Reader
        careful, careful   were you to reach
your fingers to my skin, then carve
   on through, press in – blade beneath my
breastbone (past the toothsuck, hurt)
   you'd find,

in the cool cave of my ribs,   this bloodied
          bird   my heart
is singing.

73

Postscript

What if love's not well-tooled keys and locks, glass slippers, or mutilated feet?
What if love's like tracing a silhouette in a peasouper

or like watching Polaroid paper etch itself with shades? In the slow furrow
of the nightshift hours, when workers – returning or leaving –

bruise at the edges, nod themselves back into sleep, love might keep schtum,
might speak in whiskers and bristles, jowls, spiny hair,

an awesome stink. O my godmother: for a woman to play low-stakes poker
with her friends is not, in my view, the least bit shocking.

Neither are these things call for alarm: excessive literature consumption;
making the first move. We have fallen

asleep on the back step, chins in claws, feet tucked snug, while the universe
is bearing down its icy helmet of stars.

He shifts and settles again, cranking out snore and purr, dreaming acetate reels.
How is it September already? I go inside; I leave the kitchen door adrift.

NOTES

Thirty-three (11). In his analysis of the 2011 UK riots, MP Kenneth Clarke referred to the existence of a 'feral underclass'.

Prelude (13) was written for Roddy Lumsden's Discomfort Zone event.

Stray Dog (17) was inspired by Jorge Luis Borges' *Celestial Emporium of Benevolent Knowledge*. 'Our bodies are given life from the midst of nothingness' is a quote from Yamamoto Tsunetomo's *Hagakure*, by way of the Jim Jarmusch film *Ghost Dog: The Way of the Samurai*. The man in the dog suit owes much to the Judy Budnitz short story 'Dog Days'.

In **Grizzly Bear** (20) the line 'A wicked and scandalous, infamous and immoral, bawdy and obscene song and dance, or act, corrupting the morals of the public and youth, and too filthy, obscene and immoral to be in decency further described' is taken from charges against theatre owner E.T Crall, song and dance troupe leader Palmer Hines, and dancers who had performed popular ragtime dance the 'Turkey Trot' at the Newport Theatre, Virginia, in 1912. The 'Grizzly Bear' was another popular dance of the same era. The Irving Berlin song 'Everybody's Doing It Now' was written in response to these new 'animal' dances. 'Some people talk to animals. Not many listen though. That's the problem' is from A.A. Milne's *Winnie-the-Pooh*.

Footnotes to a Long-distance Telephone Call (21) takes its name from Karin Kihlberg and Reuben Henry's 2016 exhibition of work by the Disembodied Voice research group.

The Homecoming (24) is loosely based on the story of Pertov Zalienko. Zalienko entered the US without authorisation in the 1960s and made his home in Hendy Woods State Park, California, for more than 18 years.

Wolf (25) is an affectionate response to the William Carlos Williams poem 'This is Just to Say' and to Kenneth Koch's 'Variations on a Theme by William Carlos Williams'.

Shoplifter of the World (37) was written for Alex Bell and John Canfield's 'Smithseoke' event.

Scanderoon (40) was written for a Roddy Lumsden multi-poet event. Its structure is based on *The Times*' 'Word Watching' puzzle.

from **The Blown Definitions** (43-64): These extracts are taken from a longer play for voices, written as part of a practice-based PhD.

Día de los Muertos (67) was written for Feast for the Common Dead at West Norwood Cemetery.

Pistons and Bones (68) was originally written as part of a collaborative performance by Generative Constraints at Vault Festival of Theatre.

When Glamorous Women Make Age-appropriate Dressing Statements (70) borrows from the following texts: Aviva Patz, 'Six Things That Happen When You Turn 40', *prevention.com*; Sali Hughes, 'The Secret Life of 40-year-olds: 14 things they don't tell you about the middle-aged, *The Telegraph*; Shane Watson, 'The 40 things every woman should know about fashion over 40', *The Telegraph*.